"Jeanna has a knack for helping entrepreneurs pump up their profits and have a heck of a good time doing it! This book lays out a simple system to continually increase your income and joy. It's like success on speed dial!"

— **Jack Canfield**
Author of New York Times Best Seller, The Success Principles™
and the Chicken Soup for the Soul series

"Get your Money Mind on! Sometimes getting your profit groove on requires a big mindset makeover. Other times you have to tweak your plan, systems and strategies. Luckily this book covers both in a way that's easy to implement and gets you 'fired up' to keep your profits up. It ROCKS!"

— **Dr. Joe Vitale**
Author of massive best-selling books like The Attractor Factor,
and star in the mega-hit movie The Secret

"Rock Your Profits rocks! It simplifies the most critical steps of boosting your profits so that you're no longer spinning your wheels on projects, people and systems that aren't money-makers. Plus, it delivers a big dose of mindset mojo to double your fun while you double your profits. Now that is a sweet deal!"

— **Loral Langemeier**
Author of bestseller, The Millionaire Maker

ROCK YOUR PROFITS

**STRESS-FREE STEPS
THAT TURN YOUR BIZ INTO A BADASS,
MONEY-MAKING
MACHINE**

Jeanna Gabellini

Masterpeace Publishing
www.MasterPeaceCoaching.com

Graphic Design

Victoria Vinton
CoyotePressGraphics.com

Copyright © 2018 Jeanna Gabellini

All rights reserved. No part of this book may be reproduced or transmitted in any form or by any means, electronic, mechanical, photocopying, recording, or otherwise, without the prior written permission of the author.

CONTENTS

Section I
- Tough Stuff 7
- Permission Slip for Profits 9
- Profit Fuel 11
- Optimism Gone Bad 14
- 5 Simple Steps 16
- Language 21
- Take a Chill Pill 23
- Procrastination is a Sign 25
- Prepare to Win 27

Section II
- **Profit Play #1: Own It, Baby!** 33
- **Profit Play #2: Power Up** 38
- **Profit Play #3: Inner Business Expert Hookup** ... 43
- **Profit Play #4: Vision for Wealth** 47
- **Profit Play #5: Plan for Wealth** 51
- **Profit Play #6: Wealth Plan in Action** .. 58
- **Profit Play #7: Pro or Amateur?** 62
- **Profit Play #8: Create the Vision** 65
- **Profit Play #9: "HELL YES!" Business Plan** ... 69
- **Profit Play #10: Own the Plan** 77
- **Profit Play #11: The Power of One** 80
- **Profit Play #12: Empowering Stories** .. 87
- **Profit Play #13: Game On** 90
- **Profit Play #14: Bada$$ Mode** 94
- **Profit Play #15: Show Your Trust** 99
- Boiling it Down 103
- Next Steps for Big Time Profits (and Fun!) ... 105
- Appreciation 108
- Leave a Review 109

DEDICATION

This book is dedicated to every business owner (or wannabe) who wants to easily create their money-making machine.

SECTION 1

Your Profit Foundation

TOUGH STUFF

Entrepreneurs are struggling—struggling big time.

Entrepreneurs are …

- Anxious about the future of their business.
- Spinning with overwhelm.
- Taking random actions without a winning plan.
- Looking for clarity in all the wrong places.
- Not experiencing enough freedom and fun during work hours.
- Making the profit attraction game *sooo* complicated.

If you experience any of the above, even just a little, you're in good company. Even my clients who generate multi-millions a year come to me struggling at some level with the above.

Wouldn't it be better to feel in control of manifesting your business endgame without stress?

What if you could start using fun as one of the driving forces of your success?

And wouldn't it rock if you fully trusted that your vision, plan and mindset were 100% dialed-in so that you could create a lot more money and freedom?

"Hell YES!"

It's crazy how easy it is to turn a business you love into a profit and fun machine. But most entrepreneurs don't want to stop long enough to take a step back and do the super simple things that would skyrocket their success. They're in a rut and they don't even know it.

Mind-blowing results are just a thought away. A thought away! THAT's how easy it is to create a badass, money-making machine.

Making a ton of money isn't only for super smarty pants. Prospering through your business has everything to do with your mindset, and little to do with any specific strategy.

Does strategy matter?

"Hell YES!" But it's more about how you relate to a strategy that makes it produce mega results or has it fall flat.

If you want results that blow you away, this guide will lay out a step-by-step easy process. But before we begin, open wide because I'm serving up a big dose of profit mindset. This ensures you get fat results in your business forever more.

It's time to be a badass business owner … using your authentic strengths, mindset and inspired actions to attract mega profits in a way that feels extremely fun. Like laughing-out-loud fun!

That is a badass!

People will be doing double takes as they observe your "badassery"! It's not about ego; it's about playing to your natural strengths, including your team's, and playing to win.

There is no competition when you run a business this way. Everyone will be standing in line to support you. HooRAH!

PERMISSION SLIP FOR PROFITS

I used to be the "six-figure and still broke entrepreneur" poster child. I always knew it was possible to have everything I wanted, but I was on the slow train there and couldn't get off.

I searched for a magic marketing strategy to drive more clients my way.

The harder I looked, the faster nothing happened.

The funny part (not really) was that I was coaching people on their money issues who were making millions, and even billions, but I couldn't get my business to do what I wanted. They got great results, I got very little. If only I'd taken my own advice and chilled out ... I could've been making millions long ago!

At one of my miserable financial lows (right after baby #2), I *finally* decided I'd had enough profit stagnation. It all started with that decision.

I really, really, really wanted more people to buy my services and products. Everyone who bought from me became a raving fan. So why couldn't I attract more customers?

I began making constant adjustments to my beliefs and thoughts about receiving more money through my business.

I seemed like a pretty positive person outwardly, but I did a lot of whining inside my head.

Once I became diligent about changing my business and personal paradigms, amazing things happened. Coaches and consultants magically shared their foolproof profit strategies with me. I tweaked their advice to fit my values and personality. And I wrestled up the courage to take action.

My business turned into a creativity tank. My fun factor went through the roof. Within a year I doubled my six-figure income. I repeated it the next year, too.

The better it got, the better it got.

It was so easy, that I began to fear that my success would go away as fast as it had come. I did more mindset work around believing I could sustain this winning streak. I began to trust that my business would continue to be super fun, highly creative and over-the-top profitable.

Then I began rewiring my brain about working part-time while I continued to grow my business. I've had amazing breakthroughs, and continue to push the boundaries about what I think is possible working part-time hours and generating full-time results.

Pushing my own boundaries has become one of my greatest motivators. I consider it challenging and fun to expand my capacity to let life be easy and shower me with abundance.

As you cruise through this book, expect to have more experiences of making a whole lot more money while having a blast.

This book is your permission slip to run your business in a way that tickles your fancy and puts *more than enough money* in your bank account every single day.

Money doesn't need to be a stressor. It should be something you expect to have plenty of so that you can enjoy focusing on improving the quality of what you offer and how you spend your time.

PROFIT FUEL

You're officially invited to a profit party and you're the guest of honor.

Oh, hell yes! You're about to change the way you generate money through your business. Forever.

This is a pivotal moment in your business because you're about to make a whole lot more profit, while having a whole lot more fun.

You can do this. You're totally ready.

History is not the dictator of your future.

You have the ability right here, right now, to create a business that supports the lifestyle you desire. That means your business model is wrapped around the way you want to live. If you want to work out in the morning or be able to pick up your kids at school, you can. If you like to take dozens of four-day weekends a year, it's possible. Take the summer or winter off.

You choose.

A balanced life breeds joy. And joy attracts profits!

I'm not a cheerleader. I'm a believer. Making money is relaxing to me.

Oh, I've had my share of ups and downs in the past. But the good news is that those super painful moments in my business caused me to believe at a deeper level … success is just a thought away. And that means booming profits can happen at any point in your business. They are just thoughts away!

Isn't that cool? Your mind is the one thing you have absolute control over. Not anybody or anything can get in the way of your success (so stop blaming stuff outside of you, okay?). You get to decide what happens inside your head. That's freaking empowering!

If you're super serious about getting mind-blowing results, shifting your inner game is guaranteed to lead you there. (Am I doing a good sales job to get you to focus more on inner game?!)

The purpose of this book is to show you how to boost your profits in a short time while increasing the amount of fun you experience in your business. If you're willing to slow down to devote a little bit of time each day to shifting your inner and outer profit game, then you'll see phenomenal results this year.

Crazy, over-the-top results.

Fear, doubt and shame will be gone. Poof!

This book will transform your inner profit game. My last book, *10*

Minute Money Makers: How to Easily Double Your Profits in 10 Minutes a Day gave you super easy strategies for cash infusions.

What you will learn in this book is truly the key to making ANY business strategy at least ten times more successful.

What you're about to learn will feel like driving a **brand new BMW M5** for a week after driving a 1974 Datsun B210 Coupe your whole life. It's a whole different ball game.

You see, your inner game is the most potent tool you have for making money. It drives the decisions you make, the people you attract and when/if you get sales. **It's the fuel for your money-making vehicle called a business.**

Imagine having a car without gas. You wouldn't be going anywhere, right? You'd be sitting on the side of the road while other motorists pass you by kicking up dirt in your face. No matter how fancy the car, if there's no fuel, you're stuck.

That's why you can learn slick marketing strategies, have a gorgeous website and amazing expertise and products in your niche but if your inner game isn't dialed in, you're not going to see large consistent increases in your income.

Want to double your profits and fun? Mindset, baby. Mindset.

OPTIMISM GONE BAD

I've always been a bit of an optimist, but that alone won't boost your profits.

There have been many (many!) times in my business where I've known in my gut that a new class or product was not going to make enough sales to be profitable, but I just kept chugging along and did the same old things I'd always done to generate money. And you know what happened at the end of those launches?

Not much.

But after doing the same thing over and over with lackluster results, I went from optimist to frustrated doubter. I didn't doubt the Universal Laws of Success and Attraction, I just doubted my ability to focus in a way that made those laws work for me.

I knew the right stuff to do, but I had too many of those old stories in my head making bad decisions on my behalf. Damn, little money gremlins!

They whispered a lot of really mean stuff, but here is a sampling of their main topics ...

- You're not book smart.
- You're not a good marketer.
- You're not slick and polished.
- Are you ever going to make it?
- You need a breakthrough!

- You need more money to invest in your business, then you'll get more sales.

You see why I wasn't getting dazzling results?!

Every class I taught had only 10–15% of the target number of people I wanted. I delivered transformational content week after week to only a handful of people who thought I was a godsend. But apparently I was a well-kept secret. It was beyond frustrating.

I kept up this pattern for over a decade!

I loved what I was doing, but my big fat belief about sucking at marketing was in full play. And I kept proving myself right. Based on results, I sucked at marketing.

Over the years, I proved to myself that it was easy to get private coaching clients, but I really wanted to leverage my time and make a bigger impact in the world by coaching groups. I hired marketing coaches and personal coaches. I bought books and programs. Still no breakthrough.

Then my six-figure business took a nosedive when my intimate relationship exploded. My breakup produced a stalker and I became scared. I was consumed with fear for my family, my possessions and my life.

My business was put on the back burner and six months later it was barely surviving. At some point, I snapped out of my fear and put on my CEO hat again to salvage my company.

But my profit mojo wasn't there. I had no inspiration for launching new programs. I had three clients left and that was not enough income to pay my bills. Panic set in. And my income dropped farther down the rabbit hole.

Many months later I found myself in a new relationship with a guy who owned a very successful business. My best friend's business took off about the same time.

I found it both inspiring and depressing. How come they were on top of their game while I was stuck in "Loserville"?

I visited Loserville for almost a year. It sucked to be broke but what was worse was how disempowered I felt. Like I had zero control of my outcomes. By that time, I'd maxed out my credit cards, killed my creativity and had zero confidence in my ability to get out of debt. I was tired of begging for a break. I was BEAT.

Five Simple Steps

The pain of being broke was wrecking my life.

Finally, I decided that I should stop pushing so hard for my results (DUH! I'd taught that to thousands of people!). My "pushing" energy was being driven by desperation. Desperation oozing out of a business owner's pores is stinky, right? I was definitely not going to attract new customers from that place.

My second powerful decision was to put pen to paper and map out all of my expenses and debt. I faced the financial music. It was as bad as I'd thought. But I chose to forgive myself instead of the continual self-inflicted beatings. I surrendered to my current circumstances.

That didn't mean that I gave up. I made peace with my debt, lack of funds and feeling disempowered.

I immediately felt relief. No more Loserville! **None of my circumstances had changed, just my attitude.** I felt inspired for the first time in almost two years.

Hope was ignited and I did five things that forever changed my business. I ...

1. *Got back in charge with a power move.* I made a plan to pay off debt, even though I didn't know where the money would come from.

2. *Chose one focus for my business that felt abundant.* My current clients became my #1 priority. I over delivered and felt damn happy about it. My energy shifted from not having enough clients to appreciating those I had.

3. *Developed a daily practice that built confidence.* I began organizing my home. It gave me something to focus on besides being broke and I liked feeling productive.

4. *Looked for positive evidence.* I acknowledged and appreciated every little step forward I took.

5. *Focused on transformation, not time-sensitive results.* I didn't give myself a timeline to course correct. I did what I could each day to improve my financial situation, without the pressure of a deadline. I knew it'd be worth it to change my mindset, even if it took me five years to get out of debt.

The first month my sales didn't increase, but I felt one hundred times better. Month two, I saw some small increases. And then each month the momentum built. My emotions around success and money stabilized. No more random freak-outs.

Nine months later, I was debt free. I even paid off my boat and BMW loans early! I'd also tripled my profits and hit six figures again! It felt *sooo* good. It ALL started with the conviction to get back on track and stop whining.

Those five simple steps were a winning formula, even though they seemed small at the time.

I didn't implement any new marketing strategies. I didn't create new products. I just did the five simple steps.

Each year after that, I made a little bit more money than the year before. That felt good, but it wasn't going to allow me to lead a lifestyle of freedom. I was never going to be able to retire unless I made more, saved more and worked smarter. And by this time, I was pregnant with my first son.

After my second son was born, the need to work less and make more became critical. I had some panicky moments about needing to leverage my time. I worked about 25 – 30 hours a week and I was having a hard time getting everything done.

How could I make more money only working part-time?

I had friends making seven figures and they worked about 25 hours a week, so I knew it must be possible. I just hadn't figured out how ... *yet!*

Once again, I knew the place to start was my mindset.

I began making choices like a badass, money-making CEO. I hired really smart consultants (they had results and confidence!) to teach me some of things that scared me most, like marketing. I also changed my business model and the way I communicated with my tribe.

It felt invigorating. Every change I made felt true to my personal values and brand.

My business got an injection of savvy strategies, a lot of goofiness and I was going BIG. I jumped into huge projects that felt *waaay* out of my comfort zone but I *decided* I was smart enough to pull it off (and yes, it was a decision!).

And for the finale, I decided to ask for help from my colleagues. A lot of help. I had a limiting story in my head about not wanting to bug people or put them out. It was a huge deal for me to powerfully ask people to support me in growing my business. But I'm so glad I did!

In less than a year, I doubled my six-figure income. That gave me the motivation and belief I needed to do it again the following year. And for the first time, I didn't think it was a fluke. I didn't fear that I should brace myself for a potentially bad year in sales sometime in the near future.

I trusted my ability to continually increase my income and joy.

There were some key factors to doubling my income.

I stopped …

- Rushing.
- Using the same old strategies.
- Being cheap (not investing in my business).
- Telling myself that I wasn't good at marketing.
- Acting like I had it all together when I didn't.
- Whining internally.

I started …

- Attending events to make new friends (instead of hiding out in my office).
- Reaching out to experts in my industry to pick their brains and get support.
- Expecting to exceed my desired outcomes.
- Investing in experts to help me uplevel my biz.
- Planning for immediate cash infusions *and* long-term results.
- Being more intentional about every move I made in my biz.
- Having more fun with each step.
- Acting like a CEO instead of a struggling entrepreneur.

You may or may not need to make similar changes as I did to see a radical shift in the amount of profits you attract. You're going to create your own personal recipe. Fun will be a key ingredient to increasing your profits or none of this is worth it. You get that, right?

Before we go on any further, I want to talk about the word "profit." It means the money that's left over *after* you pay expenses. I know you probably knew that, but it's interesting how many small business owners don't focus on that word when they outline their business plans.

In fact, many don't know how much money they need to make in order to be profitable. How do you know how to price your products and services if you don't know your profit goals and expenses?!

You've got to make friends with your numbers. And the numbers need to make financial sense. More on this later.

Language

Your language has a huge impact on your ability to create wealth through your business. What you speak is usually an indicator of how you feel. How you feel is generated by your thoughts.

If you want to shift into the energy of a badass business owner, change your language. It needs to be geared to the outcome or who you need to be in order to attract your outcome.

The way you communicate to yourself, others, and through your marketing can help you pump up your profits. There are certain phrases or words that can instantly increase your mojo*. When your mojo increases, your business becomes more attractive to your ideal customers.

But here's the secret to the magic of language … you have to feel it. I can say, "I'm going to have a kickass million dollar launch." But that doesn't mean squat if my emotions don't back it up.

If I say the same words while standing up, shoulders back, chest out and filled with eager anticipation, I'll feel excited to do whatever actions I need to get the job done. And it will feel damn fun!

I love words like "badass," "rockstar," and "kickass" because they energize me and compel me to step more fully into my power when I get a case of the "fraidies" (afraid that I don't have what it takes to rock my goals).

When I decide to go after a goal that scares the pants off me, I begin paying attention to my words. If I say something like, "If I do well in my launch …" I stop what I'm doing and check in with how I'm feeling about my ability to have a successful launch.

---

*mo·jo[1]
/ˈmōjō/
noun, US

noun: **mojo**; plural noun: **mojos**
1. a magic charm, talisman, or spell.
   "Someone must have his mojo working over at the record company."
2. magic power

I identify the thoughts that are squashing my belief that I will obtain my goal and change my language to, "Because my launch is going to kick ass, I am going to ..."

I feel the power of those words in my cells the more I claim them as my truth. I live into those words. I take actions that support those words.

Words are nothing without thoughts, feelings and actions to back them up. Word to your mother!

TAKE A CHILL PILL

The 15 steps (I call 'em profit plays) I've laid out aren't magic pills that produce rockstar profits overnight. It will take time for you to shift into new habits, create the ideal systems and get your profit mojo pumping. But you can change the way you perceive the process of making money to have even the nastiest anxiety and overwhelm melt away.

The more you chill out and take actions that are wicked fun, the faster you'll see badass results. Many of my clients have doubled and tripled their income in just a couple of months from using the profit plays in this guide.

In fact, if you're not having fun and digging the process of building your business, it's not worth building. Seriously. If you're not having fun you'll find yourself overwhelmed, burned out and putting out constant fires. Stress and boredom are profit deterrents.

I've seen proof with my own eyes that the process I've laid out can work for anyone. I've coached top-level management, millionaires, billionaires, spiritual healers, coaches, clothing manufacturers, artists, bookkeepers, general contractors, chefs on oil rigs and many more.

We're all born with the same resources. You have inner guidance, the ability to ask for help, the freedom to dream and the choice to take action. The profit playing field is open for you to play on.

Let go of your excuses. They're just made-up stories keeping you small. There is no fun or profits in playing to your fears.

Do yourself a huge favor and use your emotions to guide you through the process of building your business. If something you're working on feels like torture or uninspiring, question it.

- *What* about it doesn't feel good?

- Are you making up stories about the task or project that aren't true?

- Is there another way to get the job done that would feel better and get a more desirable end result?

Don't keep forcing yourself to move forward and tough it out. Suffering is not the way to reach your goals. It also causes mistakes to happen, tech glitches, and creativity blocks. And it's the best way to repel new customers and clients.

Your energy (a.k.a. your mood) is the single biggest factor in profit attraction. Strategies and systems can create small miracles in your business but not if your mindset stinks. Your energy also has a huge impact on what your team produces on your behalf. Have you ever heard the saying, "How goes the leader, so goes the team"?

You don't need to be paranoid about your negative thoughts and reactions. Just be aware of them and keep your focus tuned into a business model, plans and actions that feel aligned with what truly feels good to you.

PROCRASTINATION IS A SIGN

For over a year, my marketing guy (whom I adore) urged me to work on a marketing system that would lead people to buy my Flashpoint coaching program, where I showed my members how to build a six-figure business.

I wanted to do it because it has the potential to bring in over a million dollars a year and doesn't take much of my time. I had the outline of what I wanted to create but I wasn't inspired to get it moving.

At first I chalked it up to having a busy summer with lots of travel with my family. Then my time opened up but the marketing plan for Flashpoint still got no love from me.

I asked myself a series of questions:

- Am I creating a story that this is hard?
- Am I putting pressure on myself to get it "right" (a.k.a. perfect)?
- How can I make it easy?
- What do I need to do to allow it to feel more inspiring?

I discovered that my resistance was about choosing the content for the webinar, which was the cornerstone of the system. So I worked with my marketing guy and did some self-coaching. I called my copywriter to help with the marketing campaign, thinking that would spark a fire under my butt to take more action.

But I still didn't want to work on it, which is not usual for me.

Was I procrastinating? YES!

It wasn't inspiring! Nothing in me was screaming, "YES! I can't wait to wake up in the morning and design that webinar!" It felt painful to work on it.

What's a business owner to do?

I let it go. I didn't forget the marketing project for Flashpoint; I just put it on the back burner. I stopped pressuring myself.

I began writing this book instead. I kept feeling the nudge to get it started. I listened to that inner calling and it felt awesome to write.

A few weeks later I was hit by a new desire. I wanted a simpler business model. I wanted to further leverage my time. And guess what? The first thing that became clear to me was that I wanted to change the way I deliver that Flashpoint program. I decided to create more structure within the program, which would help the participants more easily implement the content.

Which means it's a good thing I didn't spend time and money to put a new marketing system in place only to change it a few months down the road!

I fully trusted my emotional guidance system to work on the book immediately and back burner the Flashpoint project. Trusting your inner guidance will serve you very, very well in your quest for profits.

Procrastination is a signal that begs for your attention.

It's saying, "STOP! Figure out why this doesn't feel good. Either drop this project or change the way you're perceiving or doing it."

Further into this book you're going to learn how to tap into your Inner Business Expert (Yes, you have one!), which is an extension of your inner knowing and what some call intuition.

There is no way you can become wealthy through your business without tapping into this powerful resource. You may already be using it here and there with some success. But ask yourself, "How could my bottom line benefit if I *fully* leveraged the power of infinite wisdom to which I have access?"

PREPARE TO WIN

The 15 profit plays in this book may be short and simple but they're mighty. Some are about shifting your inner game, and the others are going to take some pondering and action on your part.

If you practice the inner game strategies for a couple of weeks you're going to feel pretty damn good about your financial future. But if you practice them on a continuous basis, you're going to be living in an abundant mindset that doesn't allow stress or overwhelm to enter. Pure flow. Amazingly fun and profitable ideas will be pouring from your brain. And fun will be the name of the game.

The same goes for the strategies I'll be sharing. Implement some of them and you'll see traction in your efforts to increase your profits. Implement them consistently and your results will be staggering. You'll be able to live a life where how you choose to live and work isn't based on money. It'll be based on desire. True story.

The only reason your profits don't consistently increase is because your beliefs, focus and implementation aren't consistent (all at the same time). I know, you may think you are being consistent, but your results show you that you need to adjust something.

Maybe you need to lighten up and have more fun in your business. Maybe you need more structure. Or maybe your business model or pricing needs to be adjusted.

Maybe the one and only thing you need to change is your expectations.

Only expect to succeed. Period, the end.

When I'm creating a coaching program that I think will solve an important problem for my ideal clients, I'm super fired up to create it. I'm equally excited to map out the marketing. Wild horses couldn't stop me from taking action and executing each move with excellence.

I expect to do well financially from the endeavor but I don't really think about the money while I'm creating it. I crunch my numbers, create and implement the plan while I enjoy the ride.

I KNOW I have a winner by the way I feel. I trust that feeling and play full out. I don't hesitate or stall.

I watch many entrepreneurs say they are "all in" but in reality they have one foot on the gas and one on the brake. It's a harsh roller coaster ride of struggle and slow progress. (You're not doing that, are you?)

Whenever I teach a class or coach a client, I remind people that I'm not a business guru. I'll say the same to you. I've been coaching for over 20 years and I have a ton of proof about what works and what doesn't, to double and triple your income and fun each year.

However, you are your own best authority when it comes to choosing a business model, goals, money funnel, pricing, and marketing strategies that will work best for you.

If something doesn't feel good, stop.

Ask why and move forward in a way that feels most aligned with your desired outcomes.

The 15 lessons in this book will definitely help you get the results you want, and faster. But you have to let go of your old stories about success, money and the value you give to your customers. Trust me, you have old stories to clear out or you wouldn't be reading this. (Hell, I still have limiting stories that pop up!)

Those stories can ruin even the smartest humans. I've watched brilliant people go broke because their ego got in the way of asking for help. I've watched very talented people stress themselves out because they were afraid to slow down.

If you're serious about living the dream, go through each lesson and do the work. Sure, it'll take a few hours extra in your week. But those few hours are the difference between making a living and creating a dream.

What if you doubled your profits?

What if you nailed six figures (or seven)?

What if every element of your business felt like pleasure?

What if you became a pioneer in your niche?

And what if this was the most fun you'd ever had?

You'd be stoked!*

If you're someone who feels desperate about making more money immediately, it may serve you well to let go of a time frame entirely and focus on your desired outcome with enthusiasm while taking consistent small actions. This will increase your confidence, decrease your self-judgment and put you on the fast track to massive profits.

WARNING: Some of the profit plays in this book will seem like nice little "exercises." Yes, they will feel good, but when done in order and to completion, they form a web of profit-increasing circuits that work in harmony. They result in an entirely different way of running a business that will delight you to no end.

---

*"stoked" - adjective - to be "stoked" is to be completely and intensely enthusiastic, exhilarated, or excited about something. Those who are stoked all of the time know this; being stoked is the epitome of all being. When one is stoked, there is no limit to what one can do. – *Urbandictionary.com*

And you'll have more prosperity than you're used to having.

Want more money and fun? Then let's do this.

It's time to rock 'n roll!

SECTION 2

15 Profit Plays

Profit Play #1
OWN IT, BABY!

Whenever you want to change something in your business, you have to start where you are. You may be disappointed that you're not making more money after so many years. If you're just starting your biz you might be on pins and needles because you need to make money fast. Maybe you just quit your job and your significant other is on your back about the finances. Or you could be charging too little and working too much.

Whatever is happening in your business right now needs to be acknowledged on an emotional level. If you're not making more than enough money and totally having a blast in your business, it's having a negative impact on you. Maybe your emotions are buried deep down, but it's definitely causing an energetic upset.

Take a pause for the cause. For the sake of having more freedom and flow, check in.

What's not working for you and why?

In a moment, you're going to write a list. As you write, acknowledge how each of those things makes you feel. No more sticking your head in the sand or forcing yourself to keep forging ahead. Feel into the feelings without trying to run away.

Breathe. And acknowledge.

When I was experiencing "The Big Drought" in my business (buying groceries on a maxed out credit card and no new income in sight!), I would randomly burst into tears. I was freaked out that I couldn't pay my bills and felt powerless to change it. And it didn't help that I called myself the "Extreme Abundance Coach" in those days. How embarrassing!

I was feeling like a loser and collecting evidence of my "stuckness." I was reacting but not owning how I felt. I wasn't being proactive about a solution either. I was waiting for the "miracle idea" to fall into my lap, but it never did. I was in complete resistance to my entire financial situation.

Finally. And I mean ... FINALLY, I decided to sit down and just "be" with what was happening.

Here's how I really felt:

Shamed—I knew how to help my clients make hundreds of thousands of dollars, some even seven additional figures, but I couldn't help myself.

Scared —For the first time in my life I didn't believe in my power to attract what I wanted. I didn't know if I could break through this financial crisis. And I was contemplating looking for a job after 16 years as an entrepreneur.

Overwhelmed—My debt was growing, but I couldn't increase my income, not even by $100. I had three long-time clients paying me during this time (thank goodness!) but no new money came in, no matter what I did. I didn't see how I would ever, and I mean EVER, get out of debt.

Stressed—What if my tribe found out that Miss Abundance was broke? What if I couldn't pay my bills (sometimes I didn't)? What if I never realized my business dreams? Or lived into my potential. What if my creativity never came back?

You can see why I wasn't making any progress on my quest for profits. I was totally disempowered.

Your situation may not be as desperate as mine was, but any frustration about money or being overwhelmed needs to be cleared and released. **When you acknowledge any kind of resistance, small or big, you will open up new channels of creativity and solutions that will skyrocket your profits.**

Now it's your turn. What are you feeling about the state of your business and why? Write it down.

Then own it.

Take responsibility. Say to yourself, "Yep, this is how I'm feeling. I created my current results. Here I am. It is what it is. And so what?"

Surrender to what is. With no judgment.

So what if you've been struggling to manifest your business goals?

So what if it's taking longer than you thought?

So what if you've had to borrow money from your retirement funds or family?

So what if you're working too hard?

So what if you have fear about selling?

So what if you've been rejected?

So what if you used to make more than this in a corporate job?

So what if you're in debt up to your eyeballs?

What does it mean about you? That you weren't aligned with what you wanted. That's it. Nothing more. You're still smart, give amazing value and have what it takes to create a super fun and mega profitable business.

Life happens. To everyone.

Take some time to release any shame or drama about where you are. Breathe into it and exhale that crap out. Be with whatever emotions show up until you feel zero emotional charge about your business.

DO NOT SKIP THIS STEP. If you do, it will silently kill your business like a cancer that goes undetected.

The worst thing you can do for increasing profits is being caught up in negative thoughts and putting yourself through the wringer ... over and over.

It is, what it is. So what? Now what?

I know what. You're about to get back your profit mojo by stepping back into your power and taking control of your outcomes.

Now **that** is something to be excited about.

Ahhh ....

"My current or past circumstances don't dictate my future outcomes."

Profit Play #2
POWER UP

Now that you've neutralized your reaction about your current state of affairs in your business, it's time to heal your amnesia. Yep, you've probably been living with amnesia longer than you may be aware.

You may have forgotten things like …

- The extreme value packed in your products and services.

- The reason why you started your business and the vision that inspired that decision.

- You have special gifts that your ideal customers are longing and searching for.

- You weren't born with a business handicap. You have everything you need to kick your business into high gear.

- You're really smart.

- How to leverage your natural gifts.

- What you're really capable of. You have access to the same resources as billionaires. It all starts with mindset.

- All of the great successes you've had in your life. You've done so many amazing things, but discount them because they came easily to you. (But others would kill to have those gifts!)

- Nobody does what you do the way you do it. And that's exactly what your customers love about you.

- What it feels like to own your power and appreciate all that you've experienced up until this point.

Promise yourself right now to plug into your power. It's there. Claim it. No more pity party about not having enough time, resources, support or money.

Here's a way to boost your profit mindset …

Write down 20 things that you've experienced, produced or thought of in your business, that are clear evidence that you are a badass business owner. This step is really important. If you don't feel confident about your ability to create your business vision, than you probably won't.

Even short periods of doubt can impact your bottom line.

It's evidence that you are extremely powerful when you set your mind to it. And power is just a decision away.

Here's my list of "badassery" as an example …

1. Staying in the game when I was super broke and wanted to give up.

2. Asking Jack Canfield to be on my radio show, even when my internal gremlin wanted me to stay in my comfort zone and let the opportunity slip away.

3. Saying "YES" to Jack Canfield when he asked my BFF and me to co-author a book with him.

4. Filling my coaching practice without a website.

5. Raising my fees even though I was scared out of my mind.

6. Asking for tech help whenever I notice myself struggling.

7. Hiring brilliant business coaches and consultants that were out of my price range (who had a huge ROI).

8. Finding a way to make book number two and three fun and easy to write.

9. Changing the structure of my coaching packages when they became overwhelming.

10. Getting clients at my new rates.

11. Trusting my unconventional strategies during launches and bagging multiple six figures each time.

12. Attracting a rockstar team.

13. Working through my doubts to ask experts in my field to promote me and introduce me to other promotional partners.

14. Buying the tools I need to be more professional and make my job easier.

15. Creating structures to keep me organized so I know what to work on and when.

16. Being myself in every business interaction.

17. Learning and loving marketing.

18. Seeing each setback as a way for me to improve my business.

19. Finding creative ways to get noticed.

20. Asking how easy and fun I can make this when I'm stuck.

© Jeanna Gabellini | www.MasterPeaceCoaching.com

I just did that off the cuff and it took about 15 minutes. Wow! I feel super-duper whooper energized now.

It's so easy to focus on random tasks all day long rather than tapping into your power.

Taking responsibility for any circumstances you create in your business puts you back in your power. If you're the creator of what you have, then you can create any damn thing you want in your financial future, too. That means you're always in the driver's seat.

You're never a victim to anything or anyone. You're in control without having to be controlling.

Take a nice deep breath in and remember who you really are ... a money-making rockstar who's creating a business you enjoy. Oh, hell yeah!

If you want to further pump up your profit mojo, create a daily structure to keep you in the badass zone.

Each day write down at least five things that prove that you are on the right track towards increasing your profits. Be looking for things that may not directly be linked to money.

You can log things like ...

- Brainstorming new ideas
- Fielding inquiries from potential clients
- Connecting with a new referral source

- Finding an ideal new assistant or bookkeeper
- Writing attractive copy on your website
- Completing a task that's inspiring
- Starting a project that you've been talking about for eons.

Anything that feels like movement forward is evidence that you're on the right track. More often than you recognize, you're probably focused on your lack of progress or things that aren't working well in your business. Focusing on the things that are going well is an instant mood shifter, which will allow you to seize opportunities and create solutions lickety-split.

You can't make smart business decisions and be attractive to ideal customers when you're not powered on. So flip the switch and remember who you really are ... a profitable CEO who has a blast!

•••••••••••• ••••••••••••

"I am enough. Right now, in this moment, I have access to everything I need to rock my business!"

•••••••••••• ••••••••••••

(Stand up and say this one loud and proud!)

Profit Play #3

INNER BUSINESS EXPERT HOOKUP

There is an infinite stream of intelligence that you can tap into 24/7 so that you can be happier and wealthier in business than you've ever truly thought possible. I call this resource your Inner Business Expert.

Everybody has one, yet most entrepreneurs don't use theirs but a few times a year (and it's mostly by accident!). Why? You've been conditioned to fit into a mold. "Follow the herd. Don't trust yourself. It can't be that easy. The answers are always outside yourself."

What a crock!

Your Inner Business Expert (a.k.a. Inner or Divine Guidance) has all the great ideas, solutions, words and resources you need to kick off a six- or seven-figure income right now. Seriously. Everything you need to break into a new income bracket is right inside of you!

Awesome, eh?!

The easiest way to tap into your guidance is by slowing down.

Being in a state of chaos or focusing on checking things off your to-do list is the best way to block your ears from hearing what your expert has to say.

Take a moment now to clear your head. Get quiet, then take some nice deep breaths in and make a conscious choice to tap into your Expert. Begin by asking a question in your head or on paper.

> What's the easiest way for me to _____ [fill in the blank] _____?
>
> What's a fun way to get my desired outcome?
>
> What's the best thing for me to think or do to boost my profits?

Then listen.

Often you will get guidance by feeling a strong "YES" when something feels right. If you feel hesitant about saying "YES," don't do it until you have more information or feel more aligned with that decision.

Sometimes I ask mine specific business questions and hear an immediate answer. Other times my answer comes hours or days later (usually when I'm super attached to getting an answer *right now*!).

Another way I get advice from my Inner Business Expert (IBE) is by simply asking for guidance on what to say, do and be to manifest my ideal outcome. I also invite my IBE to help me when writing books, designing content for classes and creating marketing materials.

Once you receive your guidance, the most important thing is to trust and implement it.

Today begin to cultivate your relationship with your IBE. Use it as your #1 resource as you do the exercises and homework in this book. And be sure to use your IBE daily in your business. If your business feels hard, chaotic or unsuccessful it's a sure sign that you're not tapping into your IBE.

If you want to experience ten times the profit and fun you're currently experiencing in your business, do this …

- Set aside a half hour when you can give 100% of your attention to your IBE with no distractions.

- Go somewhere that feels relaxing and inspiring.

- Bring a notebook or laptop to capture notes.

- Close your eyes and take several deep breaths.

- Let go mentally of anything that you need to do in your future or things you've been stressing over.

- Invite your IBE to join you.

Ask the following ...

✔ What do I really want to experience in my business?

✔ What is the best thing for me to focus on to get the ball rolling?

✔ What can I practice to make it easy?

✔ Who can help?

✔ What inspired actions will make this manifest in a joyful way?

✔ Is there a game I can play to make this fun?

Notice that these questions are geared toward solution?

Then begin following through on whatever part of the guidance that felt most inspiring. Take action. Create momentum.

> ***My Inner Business Expert and I have everything we need to rock this business! I'm never alone.***

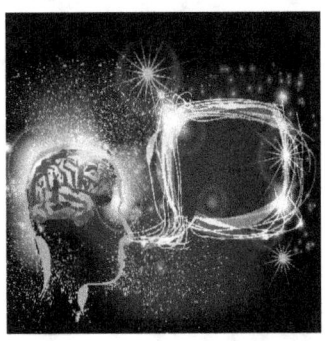

Profit Play #4
VISION FOR WEALTH

Off the top of your head, what's the coolest thing you can imagine creating for yourself in the next few years?

What would be the most magnificent thing you'd want to experience in the next five years?

Imagine what it would be like to feel well taken care of financially. Imagine feeling secure with your investments, debt, assets, home, personal needs and your future. You can now breathe easier and you feel in control of your finances.

Next, expand that picture of freedom. Imagine that you're more business savvy and you have hired wonderful people to advise, coach and mentor you. Your cash flow has increased and your perspective on wealth is more abundant and strategic. Imagine what your typical day is like as a profitable business owner. You are at ease and truly fulfilled. There's not an ounce of financial fear in your body.

Now expand the picture even farther. What are your wildest dreams about wealth and abundance? Where do you live? How do you spend your time? Who do you hang out with personally and professionally?

There are NO limitations here. This is YOUR dream. You can design it any way you'd like.

Now write all of this down in great detail, like it's a story you're telling to a friend about the transformation that you've created in your life.

There is no "right" formula here. Just get it down without editing as you go.

Notice what your gremlins (negative mind chatter) may say. They might tell you that you don't know how to execute this dream, that you're not smart enough, it's too big and lofty, it will be hard ... blah, blah, blah!

That's all an illusion. Do not buy into that crap. The key is to know that ANYONE can create WEALTH right now, if they choose to believe it, get support and educate themselves to make better choices.

It doesn't matter what your habits have been up until two minutes ago! I promise. I watch my clients go from no income to making huge deals in a matter of months after this exercise.

It may help get you started if you identify your top three to five passions. They can exist in your personal or business life. These passions make you incredibly happy or fulfilled when you focus on them.

Now imagine living out each of those passions to their max.

Allow your imagination to go to the wildest and most joyful extremes when thinking of these passions. What would that be like?

My greatest passions are family, waterskiing, teaching people to believe anything is possible and traveling. If I lived these passions to the hilt, I envision:

> *Having a vacation home on a private, waterski lake within driving distance from my home. It has several guest rooms for all of my family to stay as long as they desire. I have cars, boats, quads, scooters and bicycles for everyone. We play, dine and connect.*
>
> *I waterski almost every day and my custom boat leaves the world's smallest wake. I have several pro drivers who tow me with precision. I also have a coach teaching me how to do a waterski course like a pro. I have a dry suit that keeps me toasty on chilly days and keeps me on the water year-round.*
>
> *My coaching business keeps me jetting around the globe to be with my perfect clients for private VIP sessions and group retreats with business owners and teams. I fly first class and my family joins me often to explore the land after my coaching is complete. I take several months off each year to go on extreme adventures with my family, treating them all to dream vacations.*

I could write several pages of ideas on each passion. The vision above is actually part of my current plan and I can see the end in sight.

If you don't know how to lock into a vision that fires you up, it'll be challenging to find the drive and inspiration to rock your profits. Some people aren't motivated by money so it's even more important to know WHAT the money will give you.

If you know the desired end outcome for all that money you want to attract, it's easier to avoid the mind chatter that makes you feel overwhelmed, stressed and doubtful about the future of your business.

You've got to connect to the big dream so that you can make choices in your business on a daily basis that move you closer to living that fantasy life. Your entire business is fueled by vision.

If you're not emotionally connected to a juicy vision, how can you have the courage to be a badass profit-maker? What would make you strive to be your best self? Your vision is what makes you kick your fear in the balls!

A vision is something to live into a little bit more each day. If you have no connection to the dream, how can you create a lifestyle business? You can't. Your business becomes hard work.

Do yourself a huge favor and get your vision down on paper right freaking now. Practice *feeeeling* into it. Ask your Inner Business Expert for the inspired next steps and daily practices to step into that lifestyle now.

Passion UP, baby!

> **Writing is my greatest point of focus. When I write it like I mean it ... so shall it be.**

Profit Play #5
PLAN FOR WEALTH

Random actions lead to random results. If you want to experience wealth, plan for it. And that plan must come before you even start contemplating a business plan.

A successful business is driven by the quality of life you desire and your emotional connection to that vision. If you can't get passionate about the life you're living and the one you want to live into, how will you summon the courage to go outside of your box to get rockstar results in your business?

Money loves a plan. If you have a plan for how you're going to spend and invest your new profits, it's going be coming at ya like bees to honey. It's an energetic result from you *knowing* exactly where you're going to channel your money when it comes in.

A good business plan won't mean squat without being emotionally connected to a specific lifestyle.

Ready, set, go!

Imagine that a lot more money began to pour into your business. And then even more. And even way MORE.

How exactly would you spend it?

Would you be excited or scared that you'd lose it?

Could you trust that you'd continue to make more money each year after that?

It's time for you to step into a higher profit vibration. Everything on this planet vibrates because it's all energy. Money comes to you in direct proportion to how you feel about it. Feel wealthy and money pours in. Feel broke and it doesn't.

Creating a wealth plan will ground you in where you're headed and give you confidence about your forthcoming wealth. Planning will give you freedom because you'll make empowered decisions when the money actually begins to pour in. You won't be flying by the seat of your pants and your emotions won't trigger random choices that don't support your ultimate lifestyle goals.

You have to begin to think, plan and behave like a profitable CEO in order to be one. This plan is the beginning.

This wealth plan is more like a list of top priorities for your three phases of profit building. Those phases are …

Many moons ago, Loral Langemeier hooked me up with Robert Kiyosaki and I learned the importance of playing to win. And you can't play to win without a game plan. No more random spending, investing or reacting. Your wealth plan keeps you on the fast track to ever increasing profits and wealth.

Have you ever imagined winning the lottery and spending all that loot? A wealth plan is just like that, except it's not a long shot. You're turning wealth into a sure thing. This plan is an exhilarating process. Isn't it fun imagining how you will spend and invest a ton of money, knowing that more is coming?!

Every year you'll update your wealth plan and use it to inspire what goes on your "HELL YES" One-Page Business Plan (which you'll be doing later in the book).

You're about to create your roadmap to wealth. Here's how ...

❶ **Create your plan solo.** If you have a business partner or life partner, they can do their own plan and then you can create one together (but not necessary, contrary to what you might think). You don't even need to agree on the things you want. You are each capable of producing whatever you have in your wealth plan and you're not dependent on each other to create it.

❷ **Grab the vision you did in Profit Play #4.**

❸ **Make a list of things that need to be handled or put in place in order for you to feel financially secure.** This is the first section of your wealth plan, so write TAKING CHARGE at the top. You're taking back your power to create wealth. It's your foundation for peace. This is your life, so there are no *right* answers here except the ones that feel good.

These questions will help you choose what needs to go there ...
- How much money do you need in savings?
- What debt needs to be paid off?
- Do you need to hire a new bookkeeper, CPA, coach, or business consultant?
- What are your criteria for hiring?
- What systems need to be in place to create more flow?
- What long-term investments need to be in place?
- What do you need to learn? Who will teach you?
- Do you need to upgrade equipment, vehicles, furniture or your quality of living to feel more in the flow? (A housecleaner, assistant, landscaper or nanny can take away a ton of stress and open you up to receive more profit.)

❹ **The next section of the plan is about creating more than enough money.** Your cash flow will be increased at this level of wealth. Imagine you've doubled your income from the previous part of the plan.

What goes in this section are the things you'd want in place or to experience once you're making more than you need for necessities. You'll probably be making bigger investments, giving away more money, expanding your business and living more luxuriously compared to your current lifestyle.

You've been living in a state of security up to this point and now you're making beyond what you "need" for a peaceful existence.

Make a list of your goals for "More Than Enough."

- What do you need in order to make life simpler?
- What types of things will you be doing for pleasure?
- What type of house(s), vehicles and toys will you own?
- Who are you networking with?
- What types of systems, software, mentors, and team members need to be a part of your world so that you can have more freedom and still make a positive impact with your business?
- Do you need to incorporate?
- What other ways does your CPA advise you to shelter your pre-tax dollars?
- Are you bumping up what you put into college funds for the kids and your retirement?
- Do you want to invest in projects outside of your business?

5. **Time to prepare for extreme abundance!** Imagine manifesting massive amounts of money each year. So much money that you'd have to try really hard to spend it all in your lifetime! Imagine that you're used to making this kind of money … it's your "new normal."

You only work when inspired. You honor your values and experience the kind of freedom you only used to dream about. The sky is the limit in this section.

You may be thinking, "I don't need that much money." And you're right. But this isn't about what you need; it's about what you want. If you're feeling any resistance to imagining extreme wealth, pause for a moment and see what's triggering you.

You may have made up stories about wealthy people who are superficial. Or maybe you associate making a lot of money with a huge team or working 24/7. You may think that managing all that money will be overwhelming or scary.

This is *your* plan. Create a plan that feels damn good to YOU. You can handle large amounts of money. You can create systems and find people with expertise to help you make your finances easy and efficient. Wealth can be a burden or it can mean freedom. You get to choose.

Make a list of your goals for "Extreme Abundance."

- Who's on your team keeping things on track for your biz? For your home?
- Which new ventures have you jumped into?
- Are you a big player in a non-profit that you're passionate about?
- Do you own more property? Rent it?
- What's left on your bucket list?
- What does your investment portfolio look like?
- Any toys that you enjoy like an RV, boat, or plane?

⑥ **Check in with each phase of your plan to make sure everything you've written feels like a "HELL YES" to you.**

You want to be VERY excited about each goal; if not, axe it or change your mindset about it. Invite your Inner Business Expert to help you.

Now is not the time to figure out how you're going to accomplish each goal. You're just clarifying what needs to happen at this point.

❼ Prioritize all the goals and desires that made the cut in the "Taking Charge" section and put completion dates next to each of them. This phase may take one year or forever to complete. It's your plan, so it's your choice.

Half the fun is watching how the plan unfolds. Your job is to manage your thoughts about money and take consistent, inspired actions.

This plan is like an order form to the Universe. The people, circumstances and resources I need to bring it into reality are already being coordinated behind the scenes. My job is to begin taking inspired actions to create momentum.

Profit Play #6
WEALTH PLAN IN ACTION

Wealth is an equal opportunity activity. You've got the smarts and ability to create more than enough money to support your desired lifestyle. It's all about what you believe … so get to believing in yourself!

It's time to put that wealth plan into action and watch the moola begin rolling in, in bigger doses.

Completing your wealth plan is a lifelong adventure. For over 15 years I've been taking action and revising mine. I've accomplished dozens of things on the plan, but I also add new items each year.

As your wealth set point increases, you'll want to make changes to your wealth plan to reflect it. "Set point" means the normal rate at which you accumulate wealth. You may be receiving less money each year than you desire because you're continually thinking the same thoughts about money. Your thoughts dictate how much profit you allow into your business. If you find yourself in a rut, making approximately the same amount of profit each year no matter how much you gross, it's time to change your thoughts about money.

My wealth set point used to be very low. That's why I felt broke even when I continually increased my six-figure gross every year. My focus was on attracting a bigger gross amount each year but I never practiced a different relationship with wealth. And wealth comes from increasing profit and trusting myself to be savvy with that money.

I also found it hard to imagine bigger amounts of money consistently coming in and being able to sustain that level of wealth each year. It wasn't obvious to me at the time, but I was dragging my past struggles with profit into my present moment.

My set point was "just above broke."

Barely making enough money can feel "normal"; this is not the preferred feeling, but what you find yourself used to experiencing. It's what you expect.

A wealth plan helps you increase your set point every time you take an action step toward a goal.

The objective of a wealth plan is to inspire …

- Clarity for your business and quality of life.
- Practices which support abundance.
- New ideas and actions which lead to wealth.
- Confidence, as you see the momentum of taking small steps each month toward your goals.

Grab your wealth plan and let's get this thing in motion, shall we? Without action this plan is just a "nice" exercise instead of a vehicle for wealth attraction.

DECIDE THAT YOU WILL TAKE ACTION EVERY WEEK.

This will keep the plan alive and you'll see fast progress. The action steps don't have to be huge, just consistent. Schedule a weekly appointment with your wealth plan for 15 minutes with the commitment to taking a single action on the plan.

Maybe the first step is to make an appointment with an estate planner, bookkeeper or accountant. The next step would be to show up at the appointment. The third step would be to follow through on one action they suggest.

When I say baby steps create momentum, I mean it. You'll be amazed at what you can accomplish in the first few months of working your plan.

I STRONGLY URGE YOU TO HIRE A COACH AND/OR MENTOR TO SUPPORT YOU IN MAKING THE PLAN A REALITY.

Without all the coaching I've had in my life, I would have been blind to some very subtle, but destructive patterns I was practicing. Working through your plan requires you to trade your limiting beliefs about wealth for empowering ones.

When making important choices for your life or business, refer back to the plan.

Is the choice a fit right now? What will be the long-term impact of this choice on your wealth plan?

✔ Staying accountable to someone is key. You'll find great strength and creativity by checking in with your partners and coach every week. Be specific about inspired action each week and acknowledge any resistance you may have to following through.

✔ If you get distracted, overwhelmed or consumed by fear invite your Inner Wealth Expert to the party (yes, you have many experts at your beck and call). Most people underestimate this resource and pretend they're not smart. They look outside themselves and say, "Just show me what to do and I'll do it" or "Give me the answers." Your mind is the greatest asset you have. Use it!

✔ Get fired up about moving through the phases of this plan. Creating dreams can be scary or a fun adventure. You choose in every moment how you want to be with it. Make it a game and design the rules that inspire you to play your best.

••••••••••••••••••••••••••••••

Baby steps lead to an avalanche of wealth.

••••••••••••••••••••••••••••••

Profit Play #7
PRO OR AMATEUR?

The amount of profits you create are directly related to how you see yourself as a business owner. CEO or self-employed?

Another way of looking at how you show up in your business is by asking, "Am I acting like a pro or an amateur?"

Professionals (pros) are people who take their hobby, sport or passion seriously. They've decided they're no longer satisfied with being an amateur … somebody who likes dabbling at it but who is not "in it to win it."

Pros want the challenge and fulfillment of fully living into their potential.

And when it comes to generating a FAT profit, you can't really get there by thinking like an amateur. If your business is treated like a hobby, it will be reflected in your bank account and your level of enthusiasm.

So how does a pro think?

Pros love mastering the nuances of business that thrill them. Unlike sports, business is not a competition, so you're not trying to kill yourself winning. Pro is about being the best you can be, doing what you love as you enthusiastically pursue your wildest goals.

You can't go pro if you don't dig what you do. Can you imagine trying to be a pro downhill skier if your passion is really soccer? No! You're investing energy, time and money to create your business.

How can you be an innovator if you're not doing something you love? You can't.

PROFESSIONALS...

- Can't wait to begin their work each day. Play and work have blurred lines.

- Get the training they need, because they love expanding their skills. They like knowing what will enhance their experience or make them have an edge in their niche.

- Hire the help they need because they know they can't do it alone. Think about NASCAR racers. While we celebrate the driver who wins ... they couldn't win without their mechanics, car, coaching and sponsors. Every athlete has a coach or trainer. Everyone who has ever made it big had lots of help.

- Study their performance to learn what they can do better. They get feedback from objective sources so they can improve their game.

- Don't dabble at their passion. They're either all in or not. Being a pro is a commitment. It requires being someone who knows their power and strives to leverage their emotional intelligence.

Amateurs...

- Don't expect much to happen so they hide and procrastinate.

- Don't create plans, structures, systems or practices to win. How can you follow through with glory when you don't plan to win?

- Try random strategies without thinking about the impact on their end game.

- Don't challenge their limited beliefs.

- Live with scarcity mentally about their pricing, hiring, customer service.

- Are easily distracted and it has NOTHING to do with ADD.

Professionals can find themselves in these same habits but they recover quicker because their passion and desire to live fully calls them forth.

Everyday you have a choice ... pro or amateur?

There is only one choice if you want to easily attract big time fun and profits through your business. Choose and commit. Then get excited because going pro will make your life so much easier.

It's easier to go pro and be committed to my passion than have one foot on the gas and one foot on the brake struggling to make ends meet.

Profit Play #8
CREATE THE VISION

Profits are easy to attract when you know exactly what you want to create. It takes a badass vision. A plan. Belief in your ability to win. And constant inspired action. Repeat.

You're going to join forces with your Inner Business Expert for the following visualization to create the vision that makes going pro easy ... and profit attraction a no-brainer.

Leave your limiting thoughts and busy mind at the door. You can pick them back up when you're done (or not!). Feel free to record the following into your memo app or record on your computer so that you can play it back or have someone read it to you.

Go find a quiet and comfy place to chill. Get into a comfortable seated position and relax. You're going on a journey. This is a journey that will bring you into the future ... 12 months from now.

Close your eyes and take several deep breaths. Breathe in and out. In and out. See the air going to any place in your body that feels tense and melting it like butter. Relax your face, neck, shoulders, arms, abdomen, back, legs and feet.

Take a few more deep belly breaths, allowing any tension in your body or worrisome thoughts to be handed over to your higher power.

In your mind's eye, imagine …

◊◊◊

It is summer, one year from today. You've had a successful year meeting the goals you set out to achieve in your business. You are enjoying the season and have taken time out to reflect back on your journey.

Your life feels spacious, your bank account abundant.

- » *What is happening in your business right now that is extra pleasing?*
- » *How have you grown personally?*
- » *What's different?*

You have made some important decisions over the last year.

- » *What values do you put front and center in your business?*
- » *What are the daily practices that have helped you go pro?*
- » *Where have you invested for maximum leverage?*
- » *What have you ditched?*

> » *Who is your support team?*
>
> » *What are your favorite ways to market?*
>
> » *Which systems did you upgrade or create?*

It's awesome how you've created harmony between your personal life and business. It's like one big joyride!

> » *How do you spend a typical day?*
>
> » *What are your strengths in your business?*
>
> » *What gives you the most pleasure, zing and inspiration?*
>
> » *What does your workspace look like?*

You have tons of ideas for the future progression of your business. You appreciate all the small (and BIG) changes you made over this last year to get you to this point.

You TOTALLY trust that you will experience the essence of what you most desire in your future. There is eager anticipation for what is coming, yet gratitude for your present moment circumstances.

You've got a profitable mindset. You have clear goals and work on what feels good. You've designed a system to delegate things at work and at home that creates a seamless flow each day.

Each day you outline clear intentions for your ideal outcomes. You have easy structures for keeping track of your work, people and what you want to do in life.

> » *What do you most appreciate about the last year?*

> » *What creative marketing has helped you get to this place?*
>
> » *What partnerships and alliances have you formed that have empowered you to grow?*
>
> » *What is your annual net profit?*

You're not the only one appreciating your growth and expansion. Your business has won a major award. You were recognized in dozens of articles in newspapers, blogs and other media outlets.

> » *What were you recognized for?*

Man, oh, man! Life is getting juicer each day.

You have collected a lot of information on this journey into your future. Trust that you have everything you to need to begin creating your most profitable and fun year ... ever.

༄

Write down all the details of this vision. It doesn't have to be in order; you just want to capture the essence of what you saw in your mind's eye. Get excited. Get very excited because you'll be putting this into a blueprint that makes manifesting easy in the next step!

I couldn't have a juicy vision unless I also had the ability and resources to create it. Everything I see in my mind's eye is a sure thing when I trust.

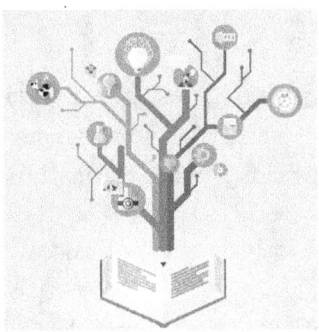

Profit Play #9
"HELL YES!" BUSINESS PLAN

If you've nailed down the essence of your vision, you've got all you need to whip out the simplest and most effective business plan you've ever created. You'll be using the one-year vision you captured in Profit Play #8 to make it easy.

Please don't cringe. I promise to make it painless. In fact, you may fall in love with this process because it's like picking out the most delicious things at the gourmet dessert (or sushi) buffet. It's only the good stuff that goes on your plate!

I've taught this planning process to thousands of clients over the years, many of them saying it was the first business plan they'd ever done.

No wonder so many entrepreneurs feel overwhelmed! It's hard to focus if you don't have a plan. Random actions usually don't lead to major increases in profit. And unless that plan fires you up, you'll never use it for guidance. It'll go in a folder that you delete five years down the road.

Plans allow you to focus on the stuff that really matters. Imagine you're driving to meet a new client who has agreed to pay you your highest fee ever. Their address is in a city that is unfamiliar to you.

What would you do if you didn't have access to a map?

You'd drive around making wrong turns and hunting down someone who knows the area.

That's what it's like trying to make more money without a plan. Even if you find someone to give you guidance to grow your business, ultimately YOU need to decide what objectives, outcomes and projects turn you on. And then you can prioritize in what order it makes the most sense to do them.

You can get help creating your business plan, but ultimately it has to resonate with every fiber of your being.

The plan you're about to create is only one page. You need to be able to look at it and see exactly where you're headed without weeding through tons of details. You can make additional detailed plans for projects if you wish, but this "Hell YES" Business Plan for your year should fit on one page.

When you're done, print it and post it somewhere visible in your workspace. You'll use it to prioritize your quarterly, monthly, weekly and daily inspired actions.

Step 1

Create your overarching theme for the year.

This theme is a kind of mantra or slogan for who you want to be in your business. This statement should get you fired up and remind you of your BIG purpose for the year.

Your theme needs to call you forward to be your best. You want it to inspire, compel and stretch you into the badass CEO you were born to be. I personally like themes with edge (but that's me).

It's your billboard for staying on track with ease, so place it at the top of your page.

Theme examples (I personally like themes that make me feel like a badass) ...

- Badass Planner
- Slow Down to Go Fast
- Seven Figure Rockstar
- Master Delegator
- Here Me Roar

Step 2

Create personal guidelines.

These guidelines will help you do what's in the best interest of your goals.

When you stay tuned to your guidelines throughout the week you'll bypass chaos, indecision and procrastination.

And when the "shizzle" hits the fan, they'll help you find your way back to what's most important.

Your guidelines are based on the way you want to think and operate to rock your profits and have a kickass time. They're not "shoulds" based on someone else's advice.

Clarify three to six guidelines, that when followed, will have a profound impact on how you lead your business. You are always leading your business somewhere (even if you're a solopreneur), so you might as well lead it to big time fun and profits.

Some of my past guidelines ...

- Appreciate every little thing.
- Think like a seven-figure CEO.
- Keep it simple and spacious.
- Don't get hung up on strategy.
- If it's not fun, don't do it.

Step 3

Create your main areas of focus.

You might have 20 things you want to manifest in your business each year and you need a way to organize them. You'll have about three to five areas of focus depending on the type of business you own and how long you've been at it.

I suggest choosing ...

- Financial
- Marketing
- Systems
- Team
- Product/Service Creation
- Practices

Under each of these will be your most energizing goals for the year.

Feel free to swap out my suggestions for something that is more of a focus for you. I've got an amazing team that's dialed in so I don't have a team focus. A couple of years in a row I had "organization" as a main area of focus. You might like to add "technical, branding" or "customer service" for your focus if that's a main priority.

It's your plan, so make it work for you. My examples of main areas of focus aren't exactly sassy or fun, so feel free to make up cool names (and send them to me) so I can make mine juicier, too!).

STEP 4

Choose a theme/mantra for each area of focus.

This is to keep your inner game aligned with your desired outcomes. For instance a few years back my theme for the financial area of focus was "Claim My Abundance!" This theme is your bumper sticker for how you want to be in this area of your business.

STEP 5

Do a brain dump of everything you want to create in your business for the coming year.

Use your answers from the process you did in Profit Play #8 in this book. Make bullet points for each thing you want, small and big.

Don't edit as you go or worry about how you're going to get it done at this point. And for goodness sake, don't listen to any bogus mind chatter judging your line items.

Your list will probably have 20 to 60 items on it. Now organize them into your areas of focus from the previous step.

STEP 6

Choose three to six of the juiciest outcomes for each main area of focus.

These are items that make you say, "HELL YES! I want to have this in the next year." They make you stoked just thinking them!

Here's an example of what an area of focus will look like with its theme next to it and goals underneath ...

FINANCIAL: MOVE INTO MY "MORE THAN ENOUGH" PLAN

1. Have $20K in business savings.

2. Create a marketing funnel to generate $25K recurring revenue a month.

3. Take 10% off the top for investments.

4. Focus on giving value and don't worry about money.

5. Plan a six-figure launch for new product.

At the end of your plan, it's mandatory to have an area of focus for "Practices." It may look something like this ...

Practices: Buddha Zen

1. Speed Dial the Universe Journal first thing in the morning

2. Email checked 2–3 times daily

3. Quarterly, monthly and weekly goals based on plans

4. Access Inner Biz Expert a minimum of once every hour

Don't worry about "how" you're going to get from point A to point B at this moment … the how's will unfold as you go through the rest of the lessons in this book and take inspired actions each day.

Right now your focus is on your end game.

One more reminder: If each outcome is a "HELL YES!" (or "Heavens YES!") and the timing to focus on it this year is a "HELL YES!" it goes on the "HELL YES!" one-page Plan!

This plan (or your version of it) is a sure sign that you've stepped into your Bada$$ Profitable CEO role more fully. Game on!

A plan in my hand allows me to prepave a profitable and fun future.

Profit Play #10
OWN THE PLAN

I **really** hope you dig the "Hell YES!" Plan you just cranked out. Most small business owners never take this step. Now it's time to put that "Hell YES!" Plan into motion and give it some life.

Most entrepreneurs think that laying out a plan of attack is what turns a business dream into a reality.

Nope.

Even if you're highly productive on a daily basis putting that plan in motion, you may still not see a huge increase in profits. I've lived that scenario several years in a row. It's very disheartening. It can be downright painful to not have enough money to pay your bills.

Make a choice to never experience the frustration, health/relationship issues and self-judgment that comes from slow sales month after month. Make a decision to never just "go through the motions" while taking actions.

Take a stand for having fun.

Breathe life into your "Hell YES!" Plan by emotionally connecting with it. You want to be able to familiarize yourself with the plan so that it feels like everything on it is a sure thing. A done deal.

If you knew without a shadow of doubt that you could experience everything on your "Hell YES!" Plan, would you ever get whacked out? Would you race around like a chicken with its head cut off? Would you think about money and get knots in your stomach or worry about the client who didn't take your offer?

Hell no!

You're a badass business owner who gets what you want, by having fun, planning and taking actions aligned with profits.

You want to see yourself as someone who can pull it off ... easily. Believe in your ability to move through one inspired step at a time to make it real. Trust that you have access to all of the resources you need to see each of your ideal outcomes come alive in Technicolor.

Here's the honest to goodness truth ...

- You know people who know people who can get you whatever you need.
- You can get the expertise, manpower and rockstar team players to make it easy.
- If you need a piece of equipment, technology, education or help, you will find the money or resources to make it happen.
- You have the ideas, solutions and creative juices to make your services and products attract your ideal customers like crazy.
- You have the gusto, commitment and expertise to soar.

- You know how to tap into the greatest resource of all … your Inner Business Expert.

Think, act and live like a badass business owner and so shall it be.

I'm not kidding when I say you gotta see yourself as a spiritually connected leader who is absolutely capable of generating a six- or seven-figure bottom line. Each year your "Hell YES!" Plan may seem overly ambitious in the beginning, but you are capable of infinite times bigger.

Everything you want is a decision away. Decide to execute your "Hell YES!" Plan with ease. Expect to have fun each day as you watch yourself come up with easy ways to get the job done.

The more inner game work you do emotionally, mentally, spiritually and physically seeing this plan as a piece of cake, the faster you will be inspired to take extremely powerful actions. And they will seem easy.

Those actions will create the momentum that will lead you to living an even better experience than you imagined.

Look at your plan daily with excitement and ask yourself, "Who do I need to be and what do I need to believe to manifest this with total ease?"

●●●●●●●●●●●●●●●●●●●●●●●●●●●●●●

I've got everything it takes to rock my plan!
I created the plan so I have the resources to
pull it off. Piece of cake!

●●●●●●●●●●●●●●●●●●●●●●●●●●●●●●

Profit Play #11

THE POWER OF ONE

The reality of being a business owner is that you have many balls to juggle ... delegating, planning, creating, tracking, following up. And if you have a small team you're probably selling, taking care of customers, creating systems, marketing, overseeing expenses and profit and so much more.

But when it comes to getting those profits to come in strong and keeping out the overwhelm, use the power of one.

One inspired profit focus at a time.

Most entrepreneurs think that offering 20 things on their menu or marketing 20 different ways will send their profits soaring. They're usually disappointed.

The reality is that you'll always have a few profit focuses at any given time. But the BIGGER reality is that if you give your intention and attention to a singular product or service for an extended amount of time, you'll produce a consistent solid earner. And that profit source will require little attention from you when you build it right the first time.

It's critical that you take the time to plan out how each product or service will become its own badass, money-making machine. You have to put systems in place for marketing, follow-up, delivery and customer service. The product or service needs to deliver on the promised end result. And all of your systems need to be tested before you roll it out to the masses.

I'm not saying wait until you have something perfected before you sell it. If you need a cash infusion, get your thing on the market. But if you want a profit machine that leverages your time, it needs some love and attention.

If you're in a hurry and slap stuff together and move on to the next thing, you haven't chosen to go pro. Slowing down is the only way to tap into ideas that blow you and the rest of the world away. You'll also want to implement those ideas with attention to detail. This is how you become a pioneer in your industry.

Wouldn't it be cool to forge new ground in your industry?

In the fun frontier there doesn't have to be blood, sweat and tears to break new ground. It should feel like the next logical step. Piece of cake!

It used to take me a couple of hours to lay out a marketing plan for a new coaching course. I was lucky to gross $15,000 for a four-month course. When I started giving the same projects six to nine months to create leading edge marketing strategies, I grossed over six figures.

Some weeks I only spent an hour working on the launch, other weeks five or six hours. Giving myself time to execute a six-figure plan turned me into a lover of marketing. It was fun brainstorming ideas with no time pressure. Having a longer time to plan also made it easier to find the right people to outsource the parts of the project in which my team didn't have expertise.

Nothing reeks of lack, like trying to rush though a project. **You can't produce abundance from lack.**

I suggest giving your brainpower to your most inspiring and potentially lucrative product or service.

Here's what you need to create success with your one inspired profit focus:

- A product or service that you wholeheartedly love selling and delivering.

- Clarify very specific outcomes for this focus. How much do you want to sell and how often?

- Make the focus be about more than generating money. What kind of transformation do you want to experience by rocking this focus?

- Work your numbers. Will the price, number of sales, and expenses support a massive increase in profits?

- It must align with your "HELL YES" Business Plan.

- Be very clear about your ideal customer and what you're promising them.

- Brainstorm and choose marketing strategies that you can sink your teeth into ("HELL YESES!").

- Identify other projects you can delegate or postpone to create space in your schedule to spend time on this profit focus.

- Decide where you need to invest money and time to go pro with this focus by improving or creating things like:

  » *Sales webpage, brochures and other marketing copy and graphics*

  » *Customer service systems*

  » *Method of delivery*

  » *Team of pros to support you*

- Tap into your Inner Business Expert and ask ...

  » *What is one of the biggest problems your ideal customers face?*

  » *How can you help? How can you make it easier for them to have their desired end result?*

  » *How can you deliver that solution in a way that feels easy peasy and enjoyable for you?*

  » *What's a solution that would feel good to deliver?*

  » *How many people would need to buy this solution in order to be uber profitable?*

  » *What's the best you can imagine happening as a result of serving this up to your tribe?*

  » *What are some unique ways of marketing it to easily*

> *grab the attention of your ideal customers?*
>
> » *What would make this project super fun for you?*

You want to think about how to knock it outta the ballpark from beginning to end.

Here's how I went from "getting by" to abundance …

I used to launch several coaching courses a year. In between courses I'd offer a special on one of my products. I honestly thought I was being smart by continually offering things up to my tribe.

I could've been rich if I ever sat my butt down long enough to dive deep into a plan to actually prosper. I was always in desperate need for a cash infusion so I did what I needed to do to make a few sales and then I hurried to the next project for my next cash infusion.

I taught one class for over 15 years and every time I launched it I made about the same amount of money, even though I said I wanted triple the amount of sales each time.

I can see in hindsight it was because I never gave the process enough thought, planning and attention. I never planned to win. And this habit was practiced with every product and service I sold.

Just because you build it, doesn't mean they will come.

Until one day …

I decided to drastically increase my average sales for a class. I chose to launch a brand new coaching course and create a very thorough plan. The mission? A six-figure launch (a pie-in-the-sky goal at the time).

Every week I booked out time in my calendar to brainstorm strategies to meet my six-figure launch goal. Every decision I made was based on this one question, "Is this what a six-figure launcher would choose?"

I was nervous because it seemed like such a HUGE goal, but I decided to play full out and have fun with it. This goal would require me to learn new things about marketing, ask for massive support and totally shift my belief about filling my coaching courses.

I saw this launch as a project that would transform who I was as a business owner and uplevel my income. And for the second time ever, I reached my desired sales goal for a course. It had been over a decade since that had happened!

Giving all that love and attention to a single focus changed the entire way I did business. That year I doubled my income and it has increased every year since then! My personal life changed dramatically, too!

No more stress about bills, taking time off or searching for the magic sales solution. My newfound prosperity allowed me to …

- Invest a ton back into my business.
- Increase monthly deposits into my kids' college funds.
- Increase monthly deposits to retirement funds.
- Build up my business savings to six figures (miraculous!).
- Hire a personal assistant.
- Give generous gifts to my team, family and friends.
- Donate to people in need and projects that enthused me.

- Buy my ideal family car.

More importantly, my confidence level went through the roof. I had huge proof that my wacky fun marketing ideas worked.

I was so used to the "hurry up because I need a cash infusion" mode. Allowing myself a longer period of time to work on one project was scary. But the payoff was huge.

I thoroughly enjoyed the planning and brainstorming process so my business mojo was pretty high. That caused my sales to increase even before the actual launch. That was a side benefit I hadn't planned on. Before and after my launch I watched products I wasn't actively marketing fly off the virtual shelves of my online business.

The more fun I had, the more my sales increased. And my creativity went through the roof. I was astounded that I could have so many profit producing ideas pouring into my head. Me, the former hater of marketing, was having a blast at it!

You will always make more money, in a shorter period of time, when you take away the pressure of time to plan a winning sales cycle (even if it feels like bankruptcy is nipping at your heels). And when you have the intent of making the process fun and enjoyable, you will have a money-maker in your offerings.

The power of focus ignites my genius and allows me to give energy to what's in my best interest.

Profit Play #12
EMPOWERING STORIES

There is only one reason why your business isn't 100 times more profitable ... your old school stories.

Stories are created by all the BS you make up about the way reality works. Reality is simple. What you believe dictates your attitude, behaviors and actions. So ultimately your financial future is dependent on your beliefs.

It's the bad news, good news.

If your beliefs stink, so will your profits. The good news is that you can change your smelly stories.

Those limiting stories will sabotage your best efforts to keep focused on that one profit project from Profit Play #11. So what's an entrepreneur to do?

Once you've chosen your one profitable focus, turn it into a challenge that calls forth the absolute best in you. Allow it to inspire you to be masterful in the areas of your business that you find most difficult.

Here is what I mean ...

When I was preparing to do my first BIG launch, I knew one of the biggest components to my success would be getting promotional partners to support it.

That made me cringe! I had to ask other successful people in my industry to invest their time and energy to promote my stuff to their people. I had three very negative stories that would ruin my efforts of ever having a six-figure launch.

First story: I would be bugging very busy people and they'd be irritated by my request.

Second story: I sucked at clearly articulating the promise of the program I was launching and they wouldn't "get" it.

Third story: I don't have time to personally ask dozens of partners to promote me.

So I did what anybody committed to getting results would do; I decided to create a new story to support my million-dollar launch goal.

New story: *I'm awesome at getting promotional partners to say, "yes!"*

I decided to get some tips on how to get partners to say "yes" to me. I began asking other people in my industry how they were successful at getting yeses. That boosted my confidence because now I had some knowledge under my belt.

From that moment on, I made decisions based on my new story. Every day I asked myself, "If I were awesome at getting promotional partners what would I be inspired to do today?"

I practiced being a business owner who asked for help from the people who could best support me.

I transformed my biggest obstacle into a learning challenge. I was tired of my old school story raining on my profit parade. My empowering story led me to believe that I could not only get people to say "yes," but that I'd find fun ways to ask them.

And people said, "yes!" In fact, more people said "yes" than "no," My new story became my new reality in a couple of months!

There was a critical component to me living into my story that I'll share in Profit Play #13.

I create stories that support my bottom line and I back it up with inspired action. BAM!

Profit Play #13
GAME ON!

Living into a new story that supports what's truly best for you and boosts your profits at the same time can be nearly impossible without a structure. Please don't cringe at the word "structure."

Structure can feel confining if you don't choose something that works for your personality style. If you make it fun, you'll stick with it and get results lickety-split.

The easiest way to do this is by turning your challenge into a game. A game can be a powerful structure for manifesting the unbelievable in record time.

Like all games, you'll need an objective and rules. Since you are creating the rules, make sure they're designed for you to win and have a helluva good time playing. I suggest adding a twist so you're challenged in a good way. Remember, you want better than average results, so that usually requires ditching your old school stories.

Your rules should stretch you into new territory that will later reward you.

In Profit Play #12, I shared the stories I made up about how it was going to be awful to ask people to support my six-figure launch. The key to my breakthrough was creating a game to ensure I took immediate action to reach out to potential partners or I'd procrastinate forever and not meet my goal.

I created a fun game to live into my new story of being awesome at getting promotional partners to say "yes" to me.

The objective of my game was to get 100 partners to say "yes."

That seemed like a crazy high amount. I didn't have time to reach out to that many people when I was trying to run my company and serve my current clients.

I believed that I could probably get 30–40 people to say "yes"; that's why I bumped it up to 100. I was going to have to go way outside of my box to do it. That objective forced me to be creative and live into my new story.

The first rule for playing my game was to reach out to five potential partners a day. Five wasn't so big that it paralyzed me, but it was enough to create momentum.

Then I thought about any old stories that would get in the way of that.

- I don't have enough time.
- I don't want be slimy in my approach.

- I don't want to bug people.
- I don't know how to clearly articulate what my program does for people.
- I don't know enough people to reach out to.

I created more game rules that would allow me to ditch those old school stories.

- Find creative ways to get people to want to hear about my launch.
- Use strategies that leverage my time.
- Have fun or don't do it.
- Ask every person I talk to, to introduce me to other potential partners.
- Get grounded and set intentions before I reach out to new partners each day.
- Go pro. No half-assing.

This game turned me into a maniac requester. I lost ALL fear after day five. I was not only asking people to support me but I became masterful at follow-up. I was EXCITED to follow up.

I used three of my highest values to make it easy: **creativity**, **boldness** and **fun**. I came up with zany and unorthodox ideas that delighted me to no end. And people responded!

Once you have your one powerful focus for profits, your new story and a game to make it real, you'll immediately get rockstar results.

What's your game? Who will play with you? How can you make it fun?

● ●

I create energizing games that lead me to rockstar profits one step at a time. I expect to win!

● ●

PROFIT PLAY #14
BADA$$ MODE

Note: This may be one of the most important lessons in this book. It paves the way for doubling your profits in a short amount of time.

There is a certain feeling you get when you …

- Have a vision or project that fires you up.
- Know that a doable and inspiring plan is in place.
- Take consistent action.
- KNOW you're going to nail your outcomes.

You feel the momentum building.

You're pumped about what's coming in the future but you're also appreciating the process of getting there.

Admit it. You feel like a badass. A rockstar. You're doing something that's going to make a positive impact in your life and the lives of your customers ... and it's freaking thrilling.

When you feel this way, mega profits can be yours. You're going beyond the "I just want to make enough to pay the bills" mindset. You're focused on being happy and wealthy. Abundant in all ways.

It will take less energy to manifest your "Extreme Abundance" section of your wealth plan than it will to manifest your "Taking Charge" section.

How can that be?

When you're focused on manifesting out of desperation, it's not fun. It's full of struggle, roadblocks and emotional sewage.

Mostly you're focused on projects in your business that come from a sense of duty, not inspiration.

When you go for the BIG HAIRY FULL OF LIFE projects you'll skip right over obstacles.

You're not worrying, you're creating.

There is no way to create bigger profits than by stepping fully into your confidence.

Nobody needs mega wealth. But why limit yourself by focusing on just paying your expenses (even though that might be a big leap for you now)?

I know that feeling like a wealthy rockstar may be a far stretch from how you feel at this moment, but with a little practice you can get there quickly. It requires "badassery."

Here are some things I have my clients do to find their Bada$$ Mode...

- Write down at least 20 things your amazing products and services give people.

- Collect testimonials from happy customers and read them often (and showcase everywhere).

- Keep a daily journal of every little shred of evidence you see or experience that shows you, "Good things are happening in my business ... size doesn't matter!"

- Ask your past and current clients what they love about you and/or what you offer. (Use this for marketing research, too!)

- Take consistent actions that will boost your mojo. (Even if they are not business related. My daily walks keep me connected to what matters most.)

- Read, watch and listen to positive stuff. (I listened to *Think And Grow Rich* more than 20 times while I was transitioning from my housecleaning biz to coaching full-time.)

- Focus on the BIG vision instead of the scary thing right in front of you. (My mission used to be "world peace one mind at a time." When I was scared to pick up the phone and ask people for their business, I'd think, "If I'm creating world peace, I'm brave enough to dial!")

- Get MAD! If you're tolerating anything less than peace and prosperity ... KNOCK IT OFF! Make a decision to be happy. SUPER HAPPY. You don't have to put up with anything less. EVER. Let that anger inspire you to take control of your mindset.

- List all of your energy drains, busy work and unprofitable actions on the left side of a piece of paper. To the right of each one decide what you're going to do about it. Immediately take action.

Bada$$ mode means you're in control without controlling. You don't have to nag, force, push, whine or manipulate to get what you want. If you do those things, it means you don't feel good enough to easily get what you want.

You already have the power to experience extreme abundance with the resources you have right now.

Go within, that's where you'll find the answers to make your next profitable decision.

You are a badass. I nicknamed one of my clients "Badass Lightworker." She was floored. She never thought of herself that way. She immediately stood taller and had a swagger to her walk.

Associating yourself with "badassery" immediately changes the way you see yourself. It crushes hundreds of limiting stories when you put "badass" in front of your title.

You are larger than life's circumstances. Everyone needs a little sass in their attitude. It's fun. Be sassy and serve millions of people their ideal solutions. Create a lovefest between you and your tribe.

When you're in badass mode you …

- Focus on the dream, not the bare minimum.
- Ask for help from the people who can help you most.
- Put your needs first. When the CEO is happy, everybody is happier.
- Lead by example.
- Trust that what you want is coming before you see any physical evidence of it.
- Tap into your Inner Business Expert.
- Come from an abundant perspective.
- Delegate like a rockstar.
- Choose pro over amateur.
- Enjoy money instead of smothering it in negative juju.
- Appreciate all that you have and all that is coming forth.
- Mind your own business! Don't worry about what anyone outside of your business is doing.
- Put FUN as your #1 business priority.

"Badassery" has infinite perks. And it feels, **oh so good!**

*I have everything I need right now
to experience extreme abundance and joy.*

Profit Play #15
SHOW YOUR TRUST

If you've taken each of the previous 14 profit plays to heart, you've set yourself up for a massive increase in your profit set point. You're expecting wealth to pour through your business and never stop.

It's time to show yourself that it's okay to leap into a different tax bracket.

Invest in yourself and your business.

Invest **time** in learning, brainstorming, planning, and executing. Invest **money** in those things, too.

If you were going for the gold, you'd do things that lead you to your edge of greatness.

Investing time and money is a sign of trusting yourself. This may be the scariest part of the journey. But it's only scary when you sit on the fence and wonder if you should take the plunge. As soon as you make a decision to jump, the entire universe conspires on behalf of your success.

You will be generously rewarded.

I can say this from experience. I've always invested before I had the money or time to do so. It knew I was making the right and perfect choice **and** I was still very nervous before I did it.

Here are some of the ways I showed my trust in my ability to be successful …

- Hired an assistant with no limit on hours.

- Set up large automatic payments for my retirement funds.

- Enrolled in a $20,000 coaching program right after buying a fixer-upper house (that needed a lot of fixing!) with no money in the bank to cover it.

- Hired a marketing person who charged double what I charged my own clients per month.

- Stopped booking appointments on Monday and Friday so that I could work ON my business or play.

- Hired a nanny, housecleaner, and personal chef so I could spend more focused time on my biz and family.

- Upgraded my systems and equipment to be pro.

Every single one of these felt like a HUGE stretch at the time. I knew each of them felt aligned with my bigger vision and yet I had anxiety before I fully trusted I'd have the money and time to do it.

Once I made peace with my choice and decided to get 100% behind it, new money came my way. I was easily able to afford them and never looked back.

Each time I upgraded my life and business, it became my new "normal." My new profit set point. I showed myself I could afford to invest the time and money to build a fun and profitable business.

I trust in the Universal Laws of Abundance. And more importantly, I trust myself.

Stop telling the world to "show you the money." The money is already there. Show yourself that you're worthy by investing in what you know will serve your highest good and big vision for your lifestyle biz.

Be open to receive support, gifts and ideal customers.

Trust your ideas and back them up with systems that will make them easy to deliver.

There is nobody else in the whole world you can trust more than yourself because you are your best authority on what turns you on. And you're connected to your Inner Business Expert and the universe.

The Source.

You will never lose when you are trusting yourself and being in the joy of creation. Prove it by saying "YES" to the things that will serve your business, even if it looks like you don't have the time or money to pull it off.

You are resourceful. You will find a feel good way to say "YES!" Take a leap of faith. Bet on yourself, because it's the one thing you have control over.

••••••••••••••••••••••••••••••

I trust in my ability to create massive prosperity by investing time and money in my business. My ROI is guaranteed when I'm aligned with my vision.

••••••••••••••••••••••••••••••

BOILING IT DOWN

Here's a quickie review of the 15 critical profit plays to more fun and profits. Skip one and you'll feel the impact (and it may not be pretty).

Sorry, didn't mean to scare you, but it's the truth.

Profit Play #1. Own it. Whatever is happening now (or in the past) with your business take responsibility for its creation. All of it. The good, and the not so good. Acknowledge any emotion and make peace with any negative mojo.

Profit Play #2. Power UP. Connect to the value that you and your company bring to your clients and customers. Acknowledge all progress.

Profit Play #3. Hook up with your Inner Business Expert. Your greatest resource is inside of you. Use it for decision-making, ideas, and clarity. Everything you need is available.

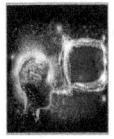
Profit Play #4. Vision for wealth. Allow yourself to articulate the big fat prosperous dream. You're not figuring out how you're going to do it, you're just letting it bubble up.

Profit Play #5. Plan for wealth. Design a game plan with action items that inspire you to break through your old stories and habits.

Profit Play #6. Wealth plan in action. Create structures and support to take consistent action on your plan. You're shifting your wealth set point through thoughts and action.

Profit Play #7. Go pro or amateur? Plan and play to win. Take your foot off the brake and step on the gas and go for the gold. Excellence is the standard (not necessarily perfect!).

Profit Play #8. Create the vision. Clarify exactly how your money-making machine is going to look and feel. Without your vision, you can't make a blueprint to get there.

Profit Play #9. "Hell YES!" Business Plan. Lay out a blueprint with your top priorities for the year, categorize them, and create guidelines to boost your mojo and keep you on track day-to-day.

Profit Play #10. Own the plan. Making a plan isn't enough. Emotionally connect to it and see this puppy as a done deal! Live into it. Act as if and so it shall it be!

Profit Play #11. The power of one. Choose to focus on one profitable project. Plan, in detail, how it will become its own badass, money-making machine. Work the numbers, know whom it serves, strategize the marketing, and dial in the action steps.

Profit Play #12. Empowering stories. Replace the old profit deflating training you've lived by and create a new set of rules that support your bottom line.

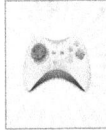

Profit Play #13. Game on! Turn your biggest challenge into a game with rules to win. This is the most fun way to turn your action into profits.

Profit Play #14. Bada$$ mode. No more forcing, controlling or whining. Change the way you see yourself as a CEO to lead your company into flow (with sass!). You've got everything you need to rock this, right now.

Profit Play #15. Show your trust. Invest time, money and energy to go for the gold. Upgrade. Leap before it's comfortable and the ROI will be massive.

Next Steps For Big Time Profits (and fun!)

I love talking about ninja marketing, online launches, team synergy, customer service, branding and pretty much any business strategy that will double and triple your income and fun. However, I didn't cover them in this book for a good reason.

If you don't take your time and do the 15 profit plays in this guide first, any other strategy I give you might be rendered useless. Once you do the steps I've outlined, everything else you do has a better chance of netting supreme results.

I have a program that teaches you how to do six-figure plus online launches without stressing yourself the hell out. I think launching is the single most profitable thing I do in my business and I can't express how fun launches are for me.

But I've watched people rush to implement the steps I share about launching and they stress out in spite of my warnings that stress and profits don't go well together. They're focused on a FAST cash infusion, not doing their best. And their launches fail.

My launch strategies flat out work. I teach my clients to adapt my launch blueprints in a way that is unique to them. But some people are more interested in the magic cash pill.

Remember: If your mindset sucks, so will your profits.

I LOVE MONEY. But I love giving value more. I love the challenge of finding fun, unique ways to positively impact my clients. I want an excellent customer service experience for my people. I care. As a result, money loves me.

Your profit game is far from over if you're having fun. Going to your office or meeting clients should be something you look forward to doing. Your business life should be as thrilling as your personal life. Retiring is for sissies (LOL!).

Seriously, fun and freedom are not things to wait for in your distant future. Practice those values now and you shall profit mightily.

Once you dial in the profit plays from this guide, it's time to put those plans into action. If you need to learn new strategies in any area of your business, please choose your mentors and consultants wisely. Check in with your Inner Business Expert before you pull the trigger. If it feels good run, do not walk, to learn from someone who is masterful and can share those tools and techniques with you.

If you need a cash infusion, read my previous book *10 Minute Money*

Makers: How to Easily Double Your Profits in Just 10 Minutes a Day. **This book is really the prequel to that one. You can grab it at** www.10MinuteMoneyMakers.com

I also have a complimentary template for doubling your profits that you can download at www.ProfitTemplate.com

For an abundance of resources to help you attract a business that provides more than enough money and joy, go to ...

www.MasterPeaceCoaching.com

Every day is an opportunity to have fun, be creative and make some money. Be kind to yourself on this journey. Appreciate what is working well, and brainstorm solutions for the things that aren't so hot.

You've got this. You're a CEO, not a small fry.

You're a badass!

APPRECIATION

I'm so happy that Rob Goyette, my marketing genius, always asks me how I can make a task easy. Because of that I see writing, launching and marketing as a highly creative pastime.

Thank goodness for coaches and consultants who share their insider secrets and bust my chops about my mindset. Without them I would've given up long ago to get a job!

My heart swells when I think about how much I appreciate the people in my life who do what they say, remind me of my brilliance and inspire me to keep rockin' it.

People that rock my world include my family, Eva, Bridget, Wendy, Mary, my clients, my team and my joint venture partners. They are abundant with their love and support. There is no way in hell I would attempt half of what I do without them.

I'm ever grateful I attended a personal growth seminar in my early twenties that introduced me to the concept that your thoughts create your circumstances. It opened up infinite possibilities in my world and turned me onto coaching. It's been an extremely wild and fulfilling ride.

And thank **YOU!**

LEAVE A REVIEW

If you were inspired and got value from this book, it would be awesome (and greatly appreciated!) if you left a review so other business owners who want to rock their profits can get their badass money-making machine into gear, too! Plus, I'd love to know ways that I can improve it, so that I can better serve you and others to experience more of what you want in your business.

Thank you!

http://MasterPeaceCoaching.com/RockyourProfitsReview